Aging

Aging

AGING

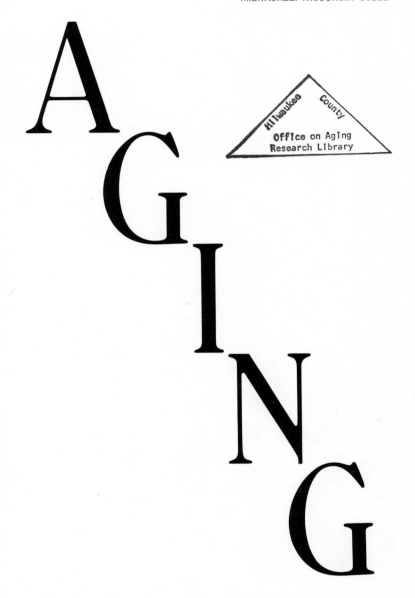
by Alvin, Virginia, and Glenn Silverstein

FRANKLIN WATTS | NEW YORK | LONDON | TORONTO | 1979

Library of Congress Cataloging in Publication Data

Silverstein, Alvin.
    Aging.

    Bibliography: p.
    Includes index.
    SUMMARY: Defines the process of aging and discusses
society's changing attitudes toward the aged.
        1.   Old age—Juvenile literature.   2.   Aging—Juvenile
literature.   [1.   Old age.   2.   Aging]
I.   Silverstein, Virginia B., joint author.
II.   Silverstein, Glenn, joint author.
III.   Title.
HQ1061.S488   301.43'5   79–11890
ISBN 0–531–02863–1

Photographs courtesy of: United Press International: pp. 5,
12, 21, 35, 57, 69, and 78; YM & YWHA: p. 30 (top); The
National Council on Aging, Inc.: p. 30 (bottom); Akron
Metropolitan Housing Authority: p. 40.

Contents

We All Grow Old   1

Do All Creatures Age?   7

The Aging Body   17

What Is Aging?   32

In Search of Lost Youth   46

Modern Aging Research   55

A World Growing Old   67

FURTHER READING   81

INDEX   83

The authors would like to thank Dr. Barbara Gastel of the National Institute on Aging for her careful reading of the manuscript and her helpful comments.

Aging

We All Grow Old

AFTER YEARS OF FAITHFUL SERVICE, YOUR FAMILY
car can no longer take the load. One part after another breaks down, and it seems that the old car is
spending more time at the mechanic's than in your
driveway. Finally, confronted with another huge re-
pair bill, your parents decide they've had enough.
They say goodbye to the old car and buy a new one.

It seems as though a car has a fixed life span. A
few old classics go purring on for decades; some fall
victim to accidents while they are still fairly new. But
most roll on, getting a little less efficient and more
prone to break down each year, until they are finally
ready for the junkyard.

The human body, too, seems to be good for only a

1)

limited life span. During childhood and adolescence we grow bigger and stronger, ever more capable and vigorous. During the middle years of adulthood, as we gather experience, we may remain strong and capable, and our minds may gain in power. But we all grow old some day. Gradually we grow weaker. The body's organs work a little less efficiently; we lose some of our appreciation of life's sights and sounds and tastes. The mind, too, may lose some of its sharpness. We become less resistant to diseases. Unfortunately, we can't trade in an old body for a new model.

How old is old? Nowadays we tend to think of sixty-five years as a dividing line. That is the age when most people can retire with full pension benefits, and until recently many companies required workers to retire at this age. But there is nothing scientific about setting sixty-five years as the boundary of "old age"—it was chosen in nineteenth-century Germany on the basis of how long it would take for a worker's payments to build up a retirement pension fund. Some people are "old" at sixty; many in their seventies would agree with statesman Bernard Baruch, who remarked (in his eighties), "To me, old age is always fifteen years older than I am."

Babies born today in the Western world can expect to live an average of about seventy-three years. But this life expectancy is not the same thing as life span. It is an average. It includes babies who die of birth defects in the first days or months of life. It includes teenagers who are killed in auto crashes and people who die of heart diseases or cancer in middle age. And, of course, it includes many people who live ten, twenty, or even thirty years longer than the average seventy-three. There are about 9,000 centenarians —people who have lived for a hundred years or more —in the United States alone, and their number is increasing each year. Modern medical advances and improved living conditions have been steadily increasing life expectancy, permitting more and more people to live to older and older ages. But so far, medicine has not been able to increase the human life span. Very few people live much past 100, and with each year above it, the number of survivors becomes smaller and smaller. An age of about 110 to 120 seems to be a sort of upper limit to the human life span.

Many people today have some mistaken ideas about aging and what it's like to be old. When they think of an old person, they think of a wizened old creature bundled up in a wheelchair in a nursing home, unable to recognize children or grandchildren, unable to remember or understand, unable to eat without aid or to control bladder or bowels—just sitting and staring into space, waiting for death. There are some old people like that, and it is a tragedy— most tragic because many of them didn't really have to become such fragile human wrecks. But these are not the majority. More people remain bright and vigorous and self-sufficient into their older years. They may have some disabilities, but they manage to compensate for them.

Take Grandma Moses, for example. Anna Mary Moses worked hard as a farmer until her late seventies. She enjoyed relaxing with her hobby of embroidering. But when she was seventy-eight, her fingers became too stiff for the delicate handling of the needle. So she began to paint in oils. People were charmed by her brightly painted pictures of rural America, and soon they were being bought by art collectors and museums. Grandma Moses was still painting actively when she died at the age of 101.

Dr. Albert Schweitzer was noted for his humanitarian work in Africa. After the first atomic explosion, he began to write and speak for peace. In 1952, when he was seventy-eight, he received the Nobel Peace Prize. Dr. Schweitzer continued to tour the world, speaking for human brotherhood until he was eighty-four. At eighty-seven he was still so vigorous that he helped build half a mile of road near his hospital at Lambaréné in Gabon; then he designed a stone bridge and helped to construct it. He was still treating patients when he died at the age of ninety.

Winston Churchill was reelected Prime Minister of Great Britain at the age of seventy-seven. Architect Frank Lloyd Wright began his most creative work at the age of sixty-nine. The construction of his last design, the Guggenheim Museum of New York, was

Grandma Moses,
shown here painting at age 98.

completed in 1959, the year he died at the age of ninety-one. Poet Carl Sandburg was still writing moving love poems in his mid-eighties. Orchestra conductor Leopold Stokowski was still making recordings of the classics in his mid-nineties.

How can some people remain so vigorous and creative in old age when others turn into human vegetables, just marking time until the end? What makes us age? Why do old people die? Can anything be done to extend the human life span?

Scientists called gerontologists are studying aging and are experimenting on prolonging life and youth. They have come up with many theories on what causes aging and many ideas on how to stop or even reverse the process. Some of these theories and ideas seem confusing and contradictory. But some seem to fit together, and gradually a clearer picture is emerging. Some researchers believe that we can unlock enough of the body's secrets to keep people young and healthy indefinitely.

Meanwhile, aging is a part of our lives, and aging people are a growing part of our world. It may seem hard to picture yourself growing old, or to sympathize with the problems that old people face. But your understanding can help to make life happier for old people in your family and community. And working to improve conditions for old people today may make it more likely that you, too, will enjoy a happy and healthy old age.

Do All Creatures Age?

THE FOREST BUZZES WITH ACTIVITY. A SQUIRREL scampers across a branch and pauses for a moment to chatter down at us. In the notch of the limb, a mother bird patiently sits on the eggs in her nest. A vine twines around the trunk of the tree, and a tangle of greenery covers the ground beneath it. In the distance we hear the howl of a wolf.

If we visit the same forest several years later, we will probably find a new squirrel scampering through the treetops and a new mother bird sitting on her eggs. The ones we saw before have grown old and died. But the same tree is there, even bigger and stronger than ever. And the same wolf is howling in the distance. It makes us wonder—is aging something that happens to some creatures and not to others? Yet the wolf is aging. Its joints are getting a little stiff, and it is no longer fast enough to hunt with the pack. It scrounges a living catching an occasional sick or injured rabbit and eating the remains of other animals' kills.

Now it is thirty years since we visited the forest. The squirrels and birds in the trees, the mice gathering seeds at the tree roots, and the rabbits crouching in the grass are all new, young individuals. The old wolf died long ago. We, too, are starting to feel the effects of age. But the tree is still living and vigorous. It will go on living after we are dead, and it will even be alive after our children are dead. Yet one day the years will finally catch up with the tree, and it, too, will die.

It seems that all of the creatures of the forest, plants and animals alike, eventually age and die. However, they don't age at the same rate or at the same time. The wolf lives longer than the squirrel. We outlive the wolf by a wide margin. And the tree is the last to go. Each kind of animal or plant seems to have its own typical life span, but eventually it ages and dies.

Are there any exceptions? Are any of the creatures of the living world immortal?

Microscopic bacteria, yeasts, and some types of protozoa seem to have an immortality of a sort. These tiny single-celled creatures feed and grow to a certain size, and then they reproduce by dividing in two. Each new "daughter" cell is a miniature duplicate of the parent cell that formed it. In turn, it can grow and divide, producing an endless series of identical offspring. Yet some protozoa cannot go on dividing indefinitely. After a certain number of divisions, the cells begin to show signs of aging. Unless they are revived by cross-fertilization with another of their kind, they eventually shrivel up and die.

In the animal world, species that can regenerate or re-form lost or damaged parts may be very long-lived. A sponge is one of the simplest forms of animals. Biologists have called the sponge "a republic of cells," for it is very much like a group of cells living together. If you pressed a sponge's body through a screen, separating it into many tiny pieces, and then suspended them in water, the pieces could join together again and re-form a living sponge. Sponges are thought to live for centuries.

Another primitive animal that lives for a long time is the sea anemone. This animal looks rather like the flower for which it was named, and it even acts like a plant. It attaches itself to a rock on the ocean bottom and never moves again. Its long, cylindrical body is topped by a fringe of waving "petals" that are actually tentacles. The sea anemone's tentacles sting tiny sea creatures and whisk them into a central mouth. The tentacles seem to have a fixed life span, and the sea anemone is continually discarding them and growing new ones. But the animal itself goes on and on.

In the 1850s, Mrs. George Brown of Great Britain

gathered some sea anemones from the coastal waters of Aran and placed them in bell jars. In 1862, sixteen of the anemones were given to Anne Nelson. She took good care of them, and they were still in good health in 1904, when they were studied by scientists. From that time on, the sea anemones lived comfortably in an aquarium at Edinburgh University, showing no signs of aging. Suddenly, in 1940, they were all found dead on the same day. The researchers never did figure out what killed the sea anemones, but from the suddenness of their death, they are sure that it wasn't old age.

Sponges and sea anemones are not very complicated animals, and they don't have much in common with humans. But there are some animals closer to us in the evolution of life that seem to be unusually long-lived. These seem to be animals that go on growing throughout their lives. The sturgeon, for example, is a fish that can continue to live and grow for a hundred years or more, showing little or no sign of aging. Turtles and tortoises, too, continue to grow throughout their lives and have extremely long life spans. One Galápagos tortoise is believed to have lived for at least 180 years.

Continuing growth seems to be the secret of the long lives of trees as well. A white oak tree can live for 600 years. The giant redwood trees of California go on living and growing for about 3,000 years. The oldest known trees are bristlecone pines, which have lived for as long as 4,600 years.

These ancient trees are the exception in the living world. Most plants grow for a few months, produce seeds for a new crop, and then wither and die. Animals, too, tend to live just long enough to ensure the survival of the next generation. The mouse, for example, has a very short lifetime. It lives only about two years. Mice can reproduce when they are just a few months old. They have large litters and they have them frequently. Within a month or two, the young mice are nearly full-grown and are able to leave the nest and live on their own.

The salmon is an even more dramatic example. For two or three years, these fish swim freely in the Pacific Ocean. Then comes a sudden urge to spawn, and the salmon begin an amazing journey. They fight their way upriver, against rapids and over waterfalls, guided by a homing instinct whose workings scientists are still trying to discover. On they swim, strong and shining. Once they enter the fresh water, they do not stop to feed. All their energies are concentrated on fighting their way back to their spawning ground, the same place where they were born. Once they have reached it, the salmon mate. Then, suddenly, the fish seem to age overnight. Within two weeks they are rotting hulks on the river bottom.

Humans and other mammals do not have as many young as a salmon, and they must provide periods of care for their young if the next generation is to survive. People don't usually start having children before their late teens, and the babies generally come one at

a time, perhaps over a period of twenty years or more. Human babies are almost completely helpless at birth, and although they gradually grow more and more self-sufficient, fifteen or twenty years of care and teaching are needed before they are ready to set out on their own. So it would seem that a lifetime of at least forty or fifty years would be needed to keep the chain of human generations going, compared with a year or two for a mouse.

In fact, humans are among the most long-lived of all mammals. Our closest relatives, the chimpanzees and gorillas, have maximum life spans of thirty-nine and thirty-six years respectively. But chimps usually live an average of only fifteen years, and gorillas average twenty-six years. There have been elephants who have lived as long as seventy years, but the average lifetime is considerably shorter. Horses live only thirty or forty years, and cats and dogs are old in their teens.

Why do some animals live longer than others? If there is a relationship to the time it takes to bear and rear young, why do some animals grow up more quickly than others? It seems as though there is a sort of inner biological clock, which ticks away at a set rate, timing the process of development from infancy to maturity and then to old age. Each species has its

Albert Schweitzer, active right up until his death at 90.

own rate of living, its own fixed life span. But what sets these biological clocks?

Gerontologists have been comparing the life spans of various animals, trying to find patterns in the rate of their development and the length of their lives. This is not as easy as it might seem. Our knowledge of the life spans of many animals is very sketchy and incomplete. Wild animals rarely live to grow old. Accidents, disease, starvation, and killing by predators or humans all take their toll. Many inexperienced young animals die before they even reach maturity. Those who do survive to raise their young may still die long before the end of their normal life spans. A rabbit getting hard of hearing would soon be caught by an owl or fox; a mountain lion whose joints were getting stiff might be unable to catch enough prey to keep itself alive. Animals that thrive in captivity usually live longer than those of their species in the wild. But even here we cannot be sure that we are measuring real life spans, since the life of an animal in captivity is an unnatural one. Still, we do have some information on life spans, and when they are compared, some interesting patterns emerge.

There seems to be a rough correspondence between size and life span. An elephant lives much longer than a horse, a horse lives longer than a rabbit, and a rabbit lives longer than a mouse. Yet there are exceptions. Small dogs and horses tend to live longer than large ones. Humans weigh much less than a horse, but we live much longer.

The general relationship of size to life span might be explained by the fact that small animals usually burn up energy much faster than large ones. A mammal is a warm-blooded animal, which keeps its body at a constant temperature. It must constantly produce energy, from the foods it eats, to replace the heat lost from the surface of its body. A tiny animal like a mouse has a much greater surface area in relation to its total size than a large animal like an elephant. So a mouse's life processes are greatly speeded up. Its heart beats about 650 times a minute. (The human heart beats about 60 or 70 times a minute, and an elephant's heartbeat rate is only about 25 per minute.) Gerontologist Albert Lansing has pointed out that the mouse and the elephant each have about 1,000,000,000 heartbeats in a lifetime. Other researchers have suggested that each animal has a lifetime quota of energy, and the various species "spend" about the same amount of energy per pound of body weight in their lifetimes. Yet there are still exceptions: in particular, humans seem to have about nine times as much energy as any other species!

Some of the exceptions disappear if we compare the weight of the brain with the weight of the body. Gerontologist George Sacher found that the larger the ratio of the brain weight to the body weight, the longer a mammal lives. Small dogs have a brain only a little smaller than large dogs. So when brain and body weight are compared, it is not surprising that small dogs live longer. Squirrels are about the same size as rats, but live much longer—a finding that becomes understandable since the squirrels have larger brains than rats. Humans, with their large brains, could be expected to have longer life spans than most other animals. There are still exceptions to this rule, though: the water mammals, the dolphins and whales, do not live as long as their large brain size suggests they should.

Why should a large brain be correlated with a long life span? Do other factors, such as the rate of energy production, play a role in setting the clocks of life? Can these clocks be reset? These are questions that gerontologists are now trying to answer through their experiments.

The Aging Body

IT WAS A PLEASANT SUMMER DAY IN MINNESOTA, and the Bubbs decided to go out blueberry picking. Cora Bubb was sixty-seven and had been living for some time with chronic health problems: arthritis and diabetes. Her husband Phil was eighty-six; he had a slow heartbeat and arthritic legs. On the way to the berry patch, about thirty-five miles from their home, their car got stuck in a mudhole. It wouldn't budge. Mrs. Bubb took her husband's metal walker and tried to walk back along the dirt road to the main highway. But her stiff and aching joints were too painful. She realized she didn't have enough strength to make it and went back to the car. The Bubbs spent a miserable night in the car, drinking coffee they had brought along and eating sugar cubes. In the morning it was

17)

raining, but Phil Bubb bravely set out with his walker to try to get help. About 2 miles (3 km) from the car, and only 150 yards (about 150 m) from the highway, Mr. Bubb collapsed. He lay there for four days, suffering through two rainstorms and swarms of biting insects. Meanwhile his wife stayed at the car, eating raspberries from nearby bushes, drinking muddy water from a marsh, and sleeping as much as she could. At last a family of berry pickers found Mr. Bubb, who told them where the car and his wife were. The next day, the Bubbs were cheerfully sitting up in hospital beds, telling reporters about their ordeal.

The story of the Bubbs makes some important points about aging. The years bring gradual changes in the body that may make it less efficient, and aging may be accompanied by various diseases and disabling conditions. But old people can still enjoy an active, full, and pleasant life, and they are often far more resourceful and tougher than most people think.

Doctors and researchers have described a number of changes in the aging body and mind. For a long time these changes were thought to be natural results of the aging process. But recently many of these views have been challenged. Gerontologists are coming to believe more and more that many of the physical losses that aging brings are really the result of specific diseases or of pressures that society places on the aging by forcing them to retire when they are used to a life of working, shunting them into old-age homes, and generally making them feel unneeded and unwanted.

More and more it is felt that some changes in the aging body and mind can be prevented and even reversed. And the aging body has ways of compensating for various losses, so that it can still go on working fairly well.

Each human being starts life as a single cell, just barely visible without a microscope. This cell divides again and again, and the mass of cells grows and develops into a baby whose body contains trillions of cells. Throughout life, cells die and are replaced by new ones. Each time you wash your hands, you rub off dead skin cells—in fact, the entire outer layer of skin is made of dead cells, which are continually lost and replaced from the layer of living cells just underneath. But some types of cells are not replaced. When cells of the brain or heart muscle die, they are gone forever. Fortunately, we start out with far more brain cells than we need, and there are usually plenty left to carry on the work of thinking and remembering. If heart cells die, leaving a tiny scar, nearby cells can grow larger and take over the load.

As a person ages, cells are replaced more slowly, and sometimes there are errors in copying cells, so that the new ones don't work quite as well as they should. In the years between ages thirty and seventy-five, the body may lose 20 to 30 percent of its cells. These tiny, microscopic losses and errors add up to produce changes in the body's tissues and organs.

Have you ever noticed an older person reading with a book held out at arm's length? A person usually

19)

starts to notice the first signs of aging when things no longer look as clear as they used to. The muscles of the eye continually change the shape of the lens, focusing it on near or distant objects to produce a clear, sharp image. With age, these muscles become less elastic, and it becomes harder and harder to focus on nearby things. Changes in the lens itself also make focusing more difficult. As the person becomes more and more farsighted, reading glasses may become necessary, usually in the middle forties. Later, brighter lights are needed to see things clearly. Cataracts may form on the eyes, blocking out vision completely. (Vision can be restored by surgery and the use of specially prescribed glasses or contact lenses to replace the damaged lenses of the eye.) Eye diseases such as glaucoma are also more common among old people and may rob them of their sight.

The changes in the eyes are only one of a series of losses of the senses that gradually narrow the old person's world. The sense of hearing becomes duller, first for high-pitched sounds and then for lower ones. Some old people begin to have difficulty making out the sounds of speech and must guess at what others are saying. Sometimes funny misunderstandings result, but gradually people with this problem become more and more isolated from the world, unless the

The great British elder statesman, Winston Churchill.

hearing loss can be corrected with an operation or a hearing aid.

Is hearing loss a normal part of the aging process? Some specialists believe that it is not, but instead is the result of all the noise that constantly batters our ears. Experiments on animals have shown that the loud electronic rock music played at discos can actually destroy the delicate sense cells in the inner ear, resulting in a loss of hearing. People in primitive tribes, who live far from the sounds of modern civilization, still have sharp hearing in their seventies.

Foods don't taste as good to an aging person. The taste buds, scattered over the surface of the tongue, normally last only a few days and are replaced. But as the years go by, this replacement slows down, until the taste buds are being lost faster than they can be replaced. By age seventy-five, a person has lost up to 64 percent of the taste buds. The sense of smell is also duller.

The aging person's senses of touch and balance also grow less sharp. Combined with changes in the muscle sense and in muscle strength, this loss of sensation makes it harder to pick up things without dropping them, and to walk without stumbling and falling.

The sense of pain also becomes dimmer with age. That might seem like a good thing. But pain is an important warning signal, which can prevent more serious injury. The pain of a hot stove makes you take your hand away before you are badly burned, and a pain in your head or body may send you to the doctor when you are sick. Without the warnings of pain, illnesses may become severe before they are noticed. This may also happen because older people are less likely to run a fever when they are ill.

Old people's systems for temperature control don't work as well as they used to. Many find it especially hard to keep warm when it is cold out and have to turn up the thermostat, bundle up in sweaters, or move to warmer climates. The body temperature of very old people may fall as low as 90 degrees Fahrenheit (32° C) instead of the usual 98.6 (37° C).

Wrinkled skin is one of the most typical signs of age. The wrinkling is caused by a loss of elasticity in the fibrous tissues, which keep young skin smooth and flexible. Aging skin is drier (the oil glands do not work as well as they used to) and spotted with brown freckles (age spots) and small black-and-blue bruises caused by breaks in fragile tiny blood vessels. Too much exposure to sunlight gradually makes the skin leathery and wrinkled. Cigarette smoking also has an aging effect on the skin.

Although extra pigment forms dark spots on the skin, pigment is lost from the hair. It gradually turns gray, then white, starting at the temples and spreading over the rest of the head. Men who have inherited pattern baldness gradually lose their hair. Some women suffer from thinning hair, too, but baldness is much less common for them. Pattern baldness usually develops only when the male sex hormone is present.

Fibers of a protein called collagen increase with

age. They grow into the body tissues and become chemically cross-linked together, forming inflexible masses. Often calcium salts are deposited around the collagen. This is one of the causes of the stiff joints of old people. The fluid that lubricates the joints also becomes thicker with age, so that they cannot move as freely.

While calcium deposits are causing problems in the joints, calcium is dissolving out of the bones, and they become brittle and easily broken. This condition, called osteoporosis, is more common among women. Although hormones and other body chemicals play an important role, the weakening of the bones by loss of calcium is also a result of inactivity. Astronauts making space flights under weightless conditions must do special exercises to keep their bones from being weakened by osteoporosis. For an aging person it can cause a vicious cycle: brittle bones and aching muscles make the person afraid to move around actively, but just sitting around makes the bones and muscles even weaker.

The cushions of cartilage between the bones of the spine gradually get thinner and flatter with age. Typically, a person loses a quarter to half an inch of height with each ten years after the age of thirty. Women lose more height than men.

Losses of cells make the muscles of the arms and legs shrink, and the muscles in general become flabbier and weaker. One study of healthy veterans of various wars showed a decrease of 29 percent in grip strength from age twenty-two to eighty-two. The heart muscle is not as efficient—at eighty the heart pumps about 30 percent less blood than it did at thirty. The muscular artery walls become less elastic and more resistant to blood flow, which may produce a rise in blood pressure. Lowered efficiency of the chest muscles and a decrease in flexibility of the lung tissue and a loss of some of the tiny air sacs may make the aging person somewhat short of breath. A loss of control over the smooth muscle that guards the exits from the bladder and bowels may result in incontinence—eliminating urine or feces whether one wants to or not.

Old age often brings problems of digestion. To some degree these may be due to faulty chewing of foods, caused by missing teeth or poorly fitting dentures. Now widespread habits of regular toothbrushing, fluoridated toothpastes or drinking water, and frequent visits to the dentist are helping more people to keep their teeth and gums healthy longer. If teeth must be removed, today's false teeth and dentures are much more effective than those of our grandparents' day. As the years go by, the stomach produces less acid, which prevents it from breaking down foods as effectively. Errors may creep into the production of enzymes needed to digest certain foods. So older people may find they can no longer eat baked beans or peanut butter without suffering from painful gas. As muscle tone is lost, the intestines may become sluggish.

With the passing years, the body needs less and

less food. For a while this may lead to overweight, as people continue eating the same amounts of foods they are used to, and their bodies store away the excess as fat. But in very old age there is a wasting of the tissues. And a failing appetite sometimes makes it a struggle for an old person to eat enough to stay healthy.

In women there is a sudden drop in the production of sex hormones during the middle years—perhaps in the late forties or early fifties. This period, called menopause, is a time of adjustment for the body. After menopause, a woman no longer produces egg cells and can no longer have a baby. But she can still enjoy an active sex life. Men don't have a dramatic menopause, but their production of male sex hormone gradually declines. Some aging men lose the ability to have sexual intercourse. Often this occurs because they expect it to, or because they believe that sex is somehow improper or "dirty" for old people.

Loss of cells takes its toll of the nervous system. Messages travel more slowly over aging nerves. The reaction time is slower. Older people tend to think things out more slowly and carefully, which sometimes makes them do poorly on intelligence tests, in comparison with younger people. (If the pressure of time is removed and accuracy is stressed, it often happens that a person's intelligence increases with age.) Sometimes older people find learning new things slower and more difficult than young people. But when they are interested and are learning something they consider important, they can learn quite effectively.

There has been some argument about the effects of aging on memory. It was thought that old people find it difficult to remember recent things and have clear, sharp memories of the distant past. These effects are probably exaggerated. When they do occur, they are probably due to the fact that we can learn and remember more easily things that are new and interesting (and few things are "new" to a person with many years of experience), and our minds tend to block out things that are unpleasant. Picture a man who is retired from his job after more than forty years of work and is living with his married daughter's family. His children and grandchildren try to be kind, but it's obvious they think gramps is "out of it," with little of value to contribute to their lives. Is it any wonder this man has trouble remembering his address? Remembering where he lives would remind him of how useless and unwanted he feels there. Yet he can remember the names of all his high school friends and (if anybody will listen) can tell long, detailed stories about the good times they had together.

Many people think that old age and senility go hand in hand. They picture the typical old person as a little dotty, unable to carry on a sensible conversation, doing foolish things—really unfit to be allowed out. Sadly, some old people do become senile, but they are a small minority. It was once thought that senility was caused by the loss of cells from the brain. But many people who are bright, alert, and intelligent in old age have lost just as many brain cells. Hardening of the arteries that lead to the brain—their gradual clogging with fatty deposits—can cut down the blood flow and starve key areas of the brain, producing damage. A stroke, in which a portion of the brain is damaged because an artery has become plugged by a blood clot or one of the blood vessels of the brain has suddenly burst, can result in the loss of some function, such as the ability to move or speak. Strokes may also lead to personality changes that may make a person appear senile. An illness may lead to mental confusion, especially if it sends the old person to the hospital, away from everything familiar and helplessly subject to the whims of hospital routine. Depression, which can happen to people of all ages, is often mistaken for senility when it strikes old people.

The growing realization that senility can have many causes has created a much more hopeful situation. When it was thought that a senile person must be suffering from brain damage, doctors and family members tended to just give up and make no real effort to help the patient regain his or her mental health. Now, better diagnosis of illnesses that might affect an old person's mind and the use of antidepressants and other drugs, as well as psychotherapy, are helping many seemingly senile patients who would have been considered hopeless in the past.

In general, gerontologists find that aging goes according to the old law, "If you don't use it, you lose it." Functions that are exercised tend to persist into old age, while those that are not gradually disappear.

People who continue with interesting, challenging work usually keep their intelligent, flexible minds. Even the deterioration of the body can be turned around to some degree. When old people are involved in carefully designed and supervised exercise, they become stronger and their organs and body functions gradually begin to work more effectively. In one study done for the Administration on Aging in 1968, a group of seventy-year-old men joined a one-year exercise program. At the end of the year, they had the body reactions of men thirty years younger.

It is said that nobody ever died of old age. But old people gradually become more and more susceptible to diseases. The typical diseases of old age—heart disease, cancer, diabetes, arthritis—are diseases that usually take a long time to develop. The gradual loss of efficiency of the body's organs and systems decreases the old person's reserve of strength to resist sudden stresses. The heart, riddled with scar tissue, may fail after a sudden exertion. The kidneys, with nearly half of their filtering units gone, may be unable to carry the extra load placed on them by hardened arteries or a failing heart. Air pollution may be too much for already weakened lungs. The immune system, which defends the body against invading microbes, gradually grows less efficient. A mild infection may overpower the body's defenders; or the defenders themselves may go wrong and turn against the body's own cells instead of attacking only foreign invaders.

During the past century, we have developed

many effective weapons in the fight against infectious diseases. Now we are making progress against such killers as cancer, heart disease, and diabetes. If we can someday cure all diseases, will we increase the human life span? Or will people just begin to truly die of old age? Can aging be cured? Or will it always be a part of our lives? Gerontologists are searching for the answers to these questions.

Above: this exercise class for the elderly, run by the YM & YWHA, is designed to help aging bodies stay flexible and firm. Below: bicycling is a popular sport for many older people, and is considered very good exercise for the heart.

What Is Aging?

WHEN A WOMAN'S SCREAMS RANG OUT IN A QUIET neighborhood in Atlanta a few years ago, the man next door didn't hesitate. Grabbing up a broom handle, he rushed over to help his neighbor. Taking her attacker by surprise, he quickly knocked him out. The police who came to arrest the burglar were surprised to find that the woman's next-door rescuer was 101 years old!

Today there are about 9,000 people in the United States alone who have reached the age of 100 or more. Many of these centenarians are still active and healthy. Some are retired. Others work part-time or even full-time. Recently the American Social Security Administration ran a survey of several hundred centenarians.

They asked these old people what they thought was the reason for their long lives. Most of their replies were included in five main types. Some said they had long-lived ancestors—parents and grandparents who had lived into their eighties or nineties. Some said they thought eating the right foods and keeping their weight down was most important. A number of the centenarians had a cheerful disposition and said they just didn't let things bother them. Getting plenty of exercise and enough sleep was also thought to be important in living a long time. And most of the centenarians in the survey said they didn't smoke, and they drank little or no alcohol.

Some years ago, scientists were excited by reports of a few isolated places in the world where there seemed to be an unusually high number of centenarians. Indeed, there were stories of many people there who were said to have lived for 130, 140, 150 years or more. These places were the mountain villages of Vilcabamba in Ecuador, the small principality of Hunza in the mountains of Kashmir, and the highlands of Georgia in the Soviet Caucasus. Gerontologist Alexander Leaf of the Harvard University Medical School visited these isolated places and studied their inhabitants. He and other researchers came up with a number of theories about why these people lived so long. Heredity might be important, they said. Vilcabamba and Hunza are so isolated that people tend to marry others of the same village. Perhaps by doing this they share an inheritance of genes for resistance to diseases.

Diet might also be important. Although the villagers in Hunza have a different diet from those in Vilcabamba or Georgia, they all eat fewer calories than we do, and less fatty foods. The active mountain life may also be important in keeping people healthy and strong. And perhaps even more important is the fact that there are no mandatory retirement ages in these isolated villages. People remain respected, contributing members of the community as long as they live.

It all sounded so logical. But now scientists believe that it was all a fairy tale. Zhores Medvedev, a noted biologist who left the Soviet Union to live in the West, has pointed out that the old people in the Caucasus are not really as old as they say. During the wars, men took their fathers' or uncles' names and ages so that they would seem to be too old to be drafted to fight. Even when the danger of having to serve in the army was over, they continued in their new identities because they were used to them, or because their seemingly great old age brought them respect.

Soon suspicions began to grow about the Vilcabambaians and Hunzukuts as well. Scientists who visited the mountain villages again after several years found that some of the centenarians they had met before were now claiming to be ten or fifteen years older than they were the last time. In 1974 a team headed by University of Wisconsin researcher Richard B. Mazess went to Ecuador to study the bones of the old Vilcabambaians. They found that some people who

*Pablo Picasso produced some of
his finest work in his later years.*

claimed to be 120 years old or more had very little osteoporosis. Their bones were like those of much younger people.

Then the researchers started checking baptismal records to make sure the people were really as old as they claimed to be. They soon discovered that many families used the same names over and over again. So it was hard to tell if the baptismal record a centenarian showed them was really his or hers, or actually that of an older relative with the same name. Sylvia Forman, an anthropologist from the University of Massachusetts, sorted out the village records and drew up family trees. When she finished, it became clear that no one in the village was actually older than ninety-six. And they had just about as much osteoporosis as could be expected for people their age.

Why do all people eventually age and die? What determines the natural life spans that seem to be characteristic of nearly all species? What is aging?

Clues to the aging process may be provided by a curious disease called progeria. People with progeria grow old while they are still children! They usually die of heart attacks or other typical diseases of old age while they are in their teens!

A typical victim of progeria seems perfectly normal at first. But after a period of from six months to three years, something seems to go wrong in the child's development. Growth slows down, the skin becomes wrinkled, and the hair turns gray or falls out. Heart trouble develops, sometimes as early as five years old but more often in the teens. Progeric children have normal intelligence, but they are usually shy and upset by the effect their unusual appearance has on other children. And they know they are doomed. They may die as young as five or six, or survive until they are nearly thirty.

Fortunately, progeria is an extremely rare condition, affecting about one out of every eight million babies born. Researchers are closely studying the few cases that occur. This condition, which an article in the *Journal of the American Medical Association* once called "Nature's Experiment in Unnatural Aging," provides a model of the aging process that develops far more rapidly than normal human aging, which would take literally a lifetime to study. But scientists are not yet sure exactly how similar progeria really is to the normal aging process, and whether they share the same causes.

Researchers have come up with many theories to explain aging. Nobel Prize winner F. Macfarlane Burnet, an expert on the immune system, says that humans and other species have a built-in "self-destruct mechanism." He believes that the aging and death of individuals is good for species, since it permits them to change and grow, adapting to changing conditions. When one generation follows another, with the old individuals continually dying away, new and different forms can appear and pass their new heredity on to future generations. Some of them may be better able to get along if their environment changes—for example, if the climate turns colder, or if different kinds of foods become available. If the old creatures never aged but lived on and on, there wouldn't be room for new forms to get established.

Other scientists believe that aging is not a part of evolution, but rather a sort of evolutionary accident. The most important time in the life of an animal or plant is the time of growing up, bearing and raising young. Changes that help to keep an organism strong and healthy until the next generation is safely raised will tend to be passed on. But anything that happens after that doesn't matter much in evolution. Since most changes in a creature's heredity (mutations) tend to have a bad effect, and only a very rare mutation makes it better, mutations making individuals less able to survive after the time of raising the young will tend to build up.

Either way, aging seems to be programmed into our genes, as a part of the overall plan of body development. Experiments by microbiologist Leonard Hayflick seem to support this idea. Hayflick grew normal fibroblasts (a type of skin cell) from unborn babies. At first the cells in the culture dishes grew and divided regularly, just as they would in the body. But then, after about fifty divisions, the cells slowed their rate of multiplication, stopped dividing, and died. Fibroblasts taken from adults showed a similar limited life span, except that they divided a smaller number of times in the cultures before they died. The older the person who supplied the fibroblasts, the fewer times the cells divided. Hayflick and other researchers tried repeating the experiments with other types of cells, such as liver cells. They, too, stopped dividing after a time. Hayflick made some calculations. It turned out that about fifty divisions is just the number of times a skin or liver cell would tend to divide in the human body in a lifetime of 100 to 115 years. So the individual cells of the body seem to be tuned to the same biological clock that governs the life span of the whole organism.

The idea of a genetic programming for aging and death agrees with the fact that each species has its own characteristic life span—for the genes determine differences between species. Genes also determine differences of one organism from another of the same species, and it is known that there are short-lived and long-lived strains within each species. That is true of humans, too: children of long-lived parents tend to live longer than the average.

Even if our life span is preprogrammed by our genes, this does not mean that we cannot hope to change it and slow down aging. University of Southern California gerontologist Bernard Strehler believes that the secrets of aging lie in the "on-off switches" that control the work of the genes. During development, genes are turned on, one after another. Each contributes its part to the building of the body, and then it is turned off, never to function again. Other genes, in-

volved in the day-to-day workings of the body, continue to function. In your body, the genes for building new skin cells and new liver cells are still turned on. If you cut or burn yourself, new skin will grow to replace what you have lost. People whose livers are damaged by disease or by drinking too much alcohol may be able to rebuild the damaged parts. But your genes for building new brain cells and new heart-muscle cells are already turned off. If you lose a part of your brain or heart, it will be gone forever. The changes in the aging body may occur because key genes have been turned off, either accidentally or as a part of the body's programmed instructions for the life cycle. If the switched-off genes could be turned on again, aging might be stopped and reversed.

How does the gene system for aging work? Scientists believe that the body's biological clock is found in a part of the brain called the hypothalamus. This region contains key control centers for many functions of the body. It controls the body temperature, the water balance, the heartbeat, blood pressure, the activity of smooth muscles, and the body's use of fats and carbohydrates. A sleep center is found in the hypothalamus, along with centers controlling the sensations of hunger and thirst, the sex drive, and the emotions of fear, rage, and pleasure. There is evidence

*Craftwork is a way for many
older people to keep their hands
flexible and their minds alert.*

41)

that the hypothalamus is important in menopause. When the ovaries of aging female rats are transplanted into the bodies of young rats, they start to secrete hormones again and produce normal eggs, which can be fertilized to yield healthy offspring. Stimulating the hypothalamus of an aging rat also sparks her ovaries to start working again.

W. Donner Denckla of the Roche Institute of Molecular Biology believes he has found the key to aging in a "death hormone" secreted by the pituitary, a gland found inside the brain. The pituitary works closely with the hypothalamus, and its hormones control the work of the other endocrine glands in the body, including the thyroid gland, which controls how fast the body burns its fuel. At the beginning of this century, it was discovered that the symptoms of the "normal" aging process are very much like those of a thyroid deficiency disease. This disease can be treated with doses of thyroid hormones, so researchers tried to treat aging with thyroid hormones, too. But the treatments didn't work. In studies with rats, Denckla has found that the problem is not the thyroid gland. It continues to secrete its hormones, but the tissues of old rats gradually lose their ability to respond to them. The researcher tried removing the old rats' pituitary gland. The operation seemed to make them younger, especially when they were given doses of thyroid hormones. Denckla has isolated a pituitary extract that blocks the action of thyroid hormone. He thinks that this is the "death hormone." If it can be purified, and researchers can find out how it works, they may be able to block its action and keep people young and vigorous.

The thymus is another endocrine gland that may be involved in aging. This gland, located near the breastbone, plays a key role in the body's immune system. It is largest and most active early in life and then gradually wastes away. As it shrinks, the thymus produces fewer and less efficient disease-fighting cells, and the body's defenders grow less efficient. Meanwhile, some of the defender-cells may begin to make mistakes. They act as though some of the body's own cells are foreign invaders and attack them. These effects are called autoimmune reactions, and they are thought to play an important role in aging. Attacks by the body's own immune defenders may be responsible for much of the loss of body cells that occurs during aging.

Some gerontologists believe that influences from the environment play an important part in aging. Radiations, chemicals that can damage genes, and temperature variations are constantly acting on our bodies and produce a kind of wear and tear. Molecular biologist Leslie Orgel of the Salk Institute for Biological Studies in the United States suggests that the information-containing molecules in cells—the genes and the chemicals they produce—gradually become blurred with errors. Genes provide the blueprints for making proteins, which build the body structures and make the chemical reactions of the body go. If the blueprints are faulty, then faulty proteins will be produced. Faulty enzyme proteins may further damage the information molecules, building up into an "error catastrophe" resulting in aging and death.

Much of the damage to the cell's molecules may be produced by very reactive chemicals called free radicals. Free-radical reactions are constantly occurring in the body, especially when oxygen combines with unsaturated fats. Denham Harman of the University of Nebraska School of Medicine believes that free-radical reactions are a key to aging. They are "like throwing sand into machinery," he says.

Free-radical reactions cross-link the molecules of the cell. Cross-linking of collagen molecules produces the wrinkled skin and stiff joints of old age. If the chemicals of the genes become cross-linked, they cannot pass on their information. Then the normal functions of the body cannot work properly.

Free-radical reactions could also produce the chemical "trash" that gradually builds up in aging cells. Particles of a yellowish "age pigment" have been observed accumulating in some cells like the junk that gathers in an attic as the years go by. In heart-muscle cells the age pigment usually takes up 6 to 7 percent of the volume in a person ninety years old, and in other kinds of cells it may occupy as much as 30 percent of the volume. Researchers are not sure what effect the age pigment and other waste products that accumulate inside cells actually have. They think that they may clog the cells and keep them from working properly.

All these different theories of aging may seem confusing. Which one is right? Actually, they may all be right, each telling part of the aging story. Many gerontologists, such as Nathan Shock, believe that aging is a very complicated process, with many causes. All these theories suggest ways to try to stop or reverse the aging process.

In Search of Lost Youth

THE GREEK GODDESS EOS, THE GODDESS OF THE DAWN, once fell in love with a mortal, Tithonus. They were married and lived together happily. But one thought kept nagging at Eos's mind and spoiling her happiness: one day her husband would die and leave her. Eos begged Zeus, the king of the gods, to give her husband immortality. Zeus granted her plea. But you have to be careful when you ask something of the gods. When Eos asked Zeus to let her husband live forever, she forgot to ask for eternal youth for him. As the years went by, Tithonus became a withered old man. He grew older and older—wrinkled and stiff, his mind muddled and wandering—and still he could not die. Finally the gods took pity on him and changed him into a cicada (a chirping insect).

Since ancient times, many peoples have feared the decay of aging and have longed for eternal youth. They searched for magic potions or mystical ways of living that would prolong life. Some thought that youth could be transferred in some way from young people to old ones. Such beliefs led to some strange practices.

In Biblical times, for example, people thought that the "breath" or "heat" of a young woman could bring new youth to an aging man. The story of King David tells how he grew old and feeble at the end of his life. He was given a beautiful young girl, Abishag, to lie with him. But the treatment didn't work. Abishag "cherished the king, and ministered to him: but the king knew her not."

Some ancient peoples thought blood had a miraculous ability to restore lost youth. Ancient Syrians bathed in and drank the blood of young people. Romans drank the blood shed by gladiators in the arena. Many centuries later, doctors tried blood transfusions from young people to old ones. In 1492 Pope Innocent VIII had the blood of three young men transfused into his veins. The treatment didn't make him younger; it killed him. In those days, nobody knew about blood types and the fact that blood from someone of a different type can cause a dangerous reaction in the body.

In China, followers of Taoism lived according to a complicated system that was supposed to bring them immortality. Ancient Taoists used a series of breath-holding exercises, trying to go back to an existence like that before birth. They ate very little, living on roots, berries, and fruits. Chinese alchemists tried a different approach to prolonging life. They tried to change the mineral cinnabar into gold. They believed that if they succeeded, they could use this noble metal to make dishes and cups, the use of which would bring them immortality. They never did succeed in changing cinnabar into gold, and neither eating from gold dishes nor holding one's breath can make an old person young again.

Many ancient myths and legends told about a fountain of youth. Its magical waters would make anyone who bathed in them immortal. The Bible mentions a river flowing out of Eden, and Psalm 36 speaks of a "fountain of life." Greek myths told of a magical youth-giving spring, in which Zeus's wife Hera bathed each year. As the centuries passed, the idea of a fountain of youth persisted. Many people read about it in the tales of the medieval writer Sir John Mandeville. Then came the Renaissance, and voyages of discovery that opened up new lands. Travelers brought back stories of amazing new plants and animals and of strange tribes of people with a very different way of life. The real wonders became blended with myths. People remembered the old tales and thought that a real fountain of youth existed, somewhere out beyond the ocean.

In the New World, Indian tribes had their own legends of a magical fountain of youth. Spanish explorer Ponce de León heard Indian stories about such a fountain on the island of Bimini in the Bahamas. Sailing from Puerto Rico in 1513, de León set out in search of Bimini and its magical fountain. He never found the fountain of youth, but he did discover the land that is now the state of Florida.

While some people chased after myths on voyages to distant lands, others searched for ways to prolong life and youth closer to home. In the sixteenth century, Swiss alchemist and physician Paracelsus claimed that he had found the elixir of life—a potion that could keep him young forever. But he died in a drunken brawl at the age of forty-eight. Luigi Cornaro, who was living in Italy at the same time, worked out a formula for living a long and happy life. He stressed eating lightly and sensibly and avoiding extremes of anything—heat or cold, overwork, and strong emotions. Cornaro's own example was a good advertisement for his theories. He remained cheerful, active, and productive until he died at the age of ninety-eight.

Cornaro's formula didn't appeal to many people. It required too much hard work. They wanted a miraculous potion or some treatment that would work immediately, without so much effort. But faith in the old magic and myths was fading. This was a time of scientific discovery and industrial development. Youth seekers now began to place their faith in science.

On June 1, 1889, the members of the French Société de Biologie heard an unusual lecture. It was delivered by Charles Edouard Brown-Séquard, a professor of physiology. Brown-Séquard was 72 years old and a noted scientist. He had published more than 500 scientific papers, and he held the chair of experimental medicine at the Collège de France.

Brown-Séquard had been observing signs of decay in his own aging body for years. As a physiologist, he was able to chart and measure the loss of his muscular strength, and he noted other symptoms of old age, such as difficulty in sleeping. His experiments on the endocrine glands and their hormones had given him an idea. Now came the startling announcement. Brown-Séquard had prepared salt-water extracts of the testicles of dogs and guinea pigs and injected them into himself. The effects, he said, were dramatic. He felt young again!

The Société members buzzed with excitement. (Their average age was over seventy, so a technique for reversing the aging process was of great personal interest to them.) The press quickly played up this intriguing story. But the scientific community greeted Brown-Séquard's report with scorn. They called him "senile" and suggested that he had imagined the good results. Researchers tried to repeat the experiments, but they had no success. Even Brown-Séquard couldn't repeat his results. His name became a joke in scientific circles. Finally he fled from Paris and stopped publishing scientific reports. His young wife left him. Five years after that fateful meeting, Brown-Séquard died of a stroke.

Brown-Séquard's idea actually wasn't a bad one. Later researchers have found that the male sex hormone, testosterone, does have a limited effect in restoring youth. But the technique the French physiologist used could not have worked. Testosterone does not dissolve in salt water. So his injections didn't contain any of the hormone.

Following up Brown-Séquard's ideas, a Viennese researcher, Eugen Steinach, tried a different approach. He tried to stimulate the body to make more testosterone by cutting the vas deferens, the tube that leads out of each testis. His treatment didn't work either. Cutting the vas deferens doesn't make the testis produce more testosterone. But it is an effective way of sterilizing a man, so that he can no longer father children. This operation of vasectomy is used by many men for that purpose today.

In the 1920s a new antiaging operation became a fad among rich old men. Serge Voronoff was a physician who had served the Khedive of Egypt before World War I. At that time, the king's harem was guarded by eunuchs, men whose testes had been removed. Voronoff noticed that the eunuchs seemed to age faster than normal. He thought that a lack of testosterone might be the reason. If removing testes could make men age, then perhaps transplanting testes could make old men young again.

Voronoff was familiar with Brown-Séquard's experiments, but he thought that the French physiologist had made a mistake. Using testes from such distant species as dogs and guinea pigs wouldn't be any good. What was needed was testes that could grow in their new bodies and produce plenty of the sex hormone. Now where could he find some volunteers who would be willing to donate their testes? There were laws against cutting up dead bodies for spare parts. Trying to get testes from criminals in prison didn't work out. Voronoff put an ad in the paper, but he got only two replies. Those men wanted so much money for their testes that the researcher gave up. He decided to use testes from chimpanzees and monkeys instead.

Voronoff worked out the surgical techniques by first doing animal transplants. In 1919 he dramatically announced his results at the Twenty-eighth French Surgical Congress in Paris. Scientists and news reporters were invited to look at several rams and a bull that had been "rejuvenated" by transplants of testes from young animals. Stories of Voronoff's "monkey gland treatment" appeared everywhere. Hopeful old men flocked to the doctor for operations at $5,000 a graft or more. Grateful patients wrote testimonials about how young they felt. But they were only fooling themselves. It is just in the past decade or so that scientists have worked out the problems of transplanting an organ so that it will survive for more than a week or two. And even now, no one can successfully transplant an organ from a monkey to a man. By the time Serge Voronoff died at the age of eighty-five, his "monkey gland treatment" had fallen into disgrace, and no one was using it any more.

Meanwhile there were other attempts to extend life and regain youth. Have you seen the magazine ads that show a little old lady from Bulgaria, standing with her little old son, both smiling their toothless smiles, while the print under the ad tells how much they like yogurt? Many people believe that yogurt helps to keep them young. They may not realize that this idea was first made popular by a Nobel Prize winner early in this century. Elie Metchnikoff had won his Nobel Prize in 1908 for the discovery of phagocytes, the white blood cells that gobble up invading germs. Metchnikoff thought that the cause of aging can be found in the large intestine, which is filled with bacteria and all sorts of harmful substances. Poisons from the intestines, Metchnikoff believed, passed into the bloodstream and damaged the body cells and organs. The Nobel Prize winner suggested two ways to eliminate the problem: either cut out the colon surgically, or change its contents so that the harmful bacteria could not grow.

As you might expect, the idea of having an operation to remove the large intestine was not very popular. So Metchnikoff searched for less drastic treatments. He discovered yogurt, a sour-milk product popular with long-lived Bulgarian peasants. The secret, Metchnikoff claimed, was the lactobacilli (milk bacteria) in the yogurt. These friendly bacteria could live in the large intestine and make it difficult for the bad bacteria to survive.

Can yogurt really keep you young? Some people

think so. But Elie Metchnikoff ate yogurt for eighteen years and then died of congestive heart failure at the age of seventy-one.

Other "miracle treatments" for aging continue to appear, become popular, and then die out. Food faddists claim that royal jelly, a special food produced by bees to feed their queen, can stop aging. But scientists believe it has no value at all. "Rejuvenation specialist" Paul Niehans treated famous people with injections of cells from the bodies of unborn lambs. Winston Churchill, Charles de Gaulle, Nikita Khrushchev, and other celebrities have flocked to Ana Aslan's clinic in Rumania. Her treatment consists of a "youth drug" called Gerovital H_3. The active ingredient seems to be the pain-killing drug Novocain. For many years, medical researchers in the West were skeptical about the reported results. But recent studies, conducted with careful scientific methods, indicate that the drug does have some effect on aging and helps to relieve depression.

Real cures for aging will not be "magic potions," or one-shot injections, or sensational surgical operations. They probably will not be discovered by the trial-and-error methods that have been used so far. Instead, they will grow out of the knowledge that comes from basic experiments on the nature of the body and how it works, through the whole cycle of development from birth to old age.

Modern Aging Research

IN 1966, IN AN ADDRESS AT THE NEW YORK ACADEMY of Sciences, gerontologist Bernard Strehler stated that the biological causes of aging could be discovered within a decade, provided that "a sufficient priority in terms of good brains, sound financing, adequate facilities, and administrative support is given this undertaking." More than a decade has passed, and researchers are still not sure what causes aging and how it can be reversed. Of course, aging research has not yet received the kind of support Strehler asked for. For example, the United States is currently spending a little more than ten cents per person per year on the support of aging research. Cancer research, on the other hand, is receiving about forty times as much, more than four *dollars* per person per year.

Now the situation is beginning to change. In 1974 the Congress of the United States passed the Research on Aging Act, which provided for the establishment of the National Institute on Aging. This new institute is coordinating and promoting research into all aspects of aging, and support for the work will almost certainly grow.

Even with the little support that aging research has received in the past, gerontologists have made some progress. They have not only gained some insights into causes of aging, but they have also explored some approaches to slowing or reversing the aging process.

A classic series of aging studies, conducted in the 1930s by Clive McCay at Cornell University, challenges our wisdom on diet and nutrition. McCay fed just-weaned rats a very limited diet. It was much lower in total calories and in proteins than the diet the animals would prefer if they were allowed to eat their fill. The young rats grew and matured more slowly than littermates that were fed a normal diet. But they lived up to 100 percent longer.

More recent studies have expanded this landmark work. It has been found that the amount of protein in the diet is especially important. D. S. Miller and P. R. Payne, for example, increased the lifetime of

The great American poet
Carl Sandburg, at age 85.

rats by feeding them a high-protein diet for the first four months of life after birth and then a very low-protein diet afterward. Other researchers have used low-protein, low-calorie diets from the time of weaning onward. Researchers at the Monsanto Corporation found that the lives of chicks and mice could be lengthened by feeding them a diet lacking just one essential amino acid, tryptophan. (Amino acids are the building blocks of proteins.)

The implications of these experiments are startling. Modern parents try to feed their children as well as possible and feel proud as their babies steadily gain weight. Children are growing faster and bigger than they did a generation or two ago, and we generally regard this as a sign of health. But might they live longer if they didn't eat as well and grew more slowly?

It's hard to say how much these feeding experiments should be extended to humans. Tampering with children's diets could be very dangerous. In Miller and Payne's experiments, for example, rats that grew on some variations of the limited diets were sickly. On other diets they appeared healthy, but they were sterile—they could not produce living young. On still other diets, the rats were healthy but undersized. Cutting down too severely on calories and, in particular, on proteins can stunt the physical and mental development of children. Yet overfeeding is not healthy either. We need more studies to show us what to do. Meanwhile, gerontologists are speculating on just how a limited diet works in prolonging the lives of experimental animals.

Some researchers have argued that limiting the diet of young rats does not really affect the aging process itself. Instead, it prevents or postpones the lung and kidney diseases that normally kill rats. The increase in lifetime produced in the diet experiments is thus similar to the increase in human life expectancy that occurred when diseases such as diphtheria were wiped out. However, there is some evidence that limiting the diet may actually delay aging by working through the immune system. Roy Walford and Richard Liu of the School of Medicine of the University of California at Los Angeles have found that a low-calorie, low-protein diet slows down the maturing of the immune system in young mice. When they are young they have a low resistance to disease germs. But when they get older, their immune system actually works better than in mice fed a normal diet. Walford suggests that slowing down the development of the immune system early in life may delay the appearance of auto-antibodies—defenders that would attack the body's own cells by mistake. These auto-antibodies are thought by some researchers to be an important part of the aging process.

In the future, when people go to bed at night, they may use electric blankets to cool, rather than to warm themselves. Experiments on fish and other animals have shown that lowering the body temperature lengthens life. Scientists thought that this effect is due to a general slowing down of body processes by the cooler temperatures—a slowing of the biological clock that ticks away a measured life span. But new studies suggest that the immune system may be involved here, too. When fish were kept at temperatures about 5 degrees Celsius below normal, they grew normally and eventually grew even larger than fish raised at the normal temperature. But cooling decreased the response of their immune system.

Investigations of the body's biological clock and the hormones that govern body processes are providing some interesting approaches to extending life. Paola S. Timiras of the University of California at Berkeley has been studying the brain. She believes that the nerve transmitter chemical, serotonin, may be the trigger that causes the hypothalamus and pituitary to release the "death hormone" that may contribute to aging. The amount of serotonin in the brain increases with age. This theory agrees well with the diet experiments in which the lives of animals were extended by decreasing the amount of tryptophan in the diet. Tryptophan and serotonin are very similar chemically, and in the body serotonin is made from tryptophan.

In other experiments, researchers have tried linking the bloodstreams of a young animal and an old animal. This kind of experiment is called parabiosis. At GRC/Baltimore, Dietrich Bodenstein created Siamese-twin cockroaches by parabiosis, with a young roach joined to an old one. (They were connected in such a way that they could run around freely and live quite normally.) Young cockroaches can readily grow back a lost limb, but old ones lose this ability. In the parabiotic pairs, the old roach recovered its powers of regeneration. When the researcher cut off a limb, it promptly grew back.

Insects have a hormone called juvenile hormone, which keeps them in an immature form. Bodenstein thought that juvenile hormone from the young roach was being transmitted through the joined bloodstream to the old roach. But several years later, Frederic C. Ludwig of the University of California at Irvine conducted similar experiments on rats. A young rat and an old rat were joined tail-to-shoulder. The rats were from a carefully inbred strain, so that their heredity was almost as alike as that of identical twins. The effect of parabiosis on the old rats was dramatic. Their blood cholesterol levels fell, and other changes made their bodies younger. They went on living long beyond their normal life span, and long after their normal littermates were dead. Scientists have not yet found any hormone in rats that would correspond to the juvenile hormone in insects. Could some still unknown hormone be passing from the blood of the young rats into that of their old parabiotic "twins"? Or could it be that the blood of the younger rats just diluted the "death hormone," or their bodies destroyed or disposed of it, so that it did not have its effect on the older rats? Researchers at several laboratories are now trying to find out.

The thymus gland is another promising target for aging research. A National Institutes of Health team headed by Takashi Makinodan has transplanted thymuses and bone marrow from young mice into older ones. The immune systems of nineteen-month-old mice became just as effective as those of four-month-old mice. If mice were people, the subjects of these experiments would have been sixty-year-olds, whose immune systems were made as young as those of twenty-year-olds. Some of the experimental mice lived about one-third beyond their normal life span. This was all the more amazing because during that time a serious virus epidemic swept through the laboratory, killing many of the 9,000 mice in the research colony.

Transplanting whole thymus glands may not be necessary. The thymus produces a mixture of hormones called thymosin. University of Texas researchers have found that the levels of thymosin in the blood fall sharply with age. Thymosin injections might be just as effective as thymus transplants in halting the aging process.

The theories on the role of free-radical reactions in aging are also providing fruitful starting points for research. Denham Harman has raised mice and rats on diets containing a variety of fats and found that the animals whose diets were lower in unsaturated fats had longer life spans. (Remember that reactions between unsaturated fats and oxygen are free-radical reactions.) This finding is rather disturbing. For many years, heart specialists have been urging people to eat less saturated fats, such as butter and the fat on meat, and replace them with unsaturated fats, such as corn oil. This seemed to be good advice, for the fatty deposits that clog up arteries and lead to heart attacks and strokes are made from saturated fats. But now it seems that too much unsaturated fat in the diet may be even worse. In addition to the studies suggesting that unsaturated fats may lead to aging, there have been indications that free-radical reactions may also be important in causing cancer. And some researchers even believe that damage due to free-radical reactions may be what gets the fatty deposits inside arteries started. Probably the safest thing to do is to cut down on the amount of *all* fats in the diet. A certain amount of fat is necessary for good health. But there is little doubt that most Westerners are now eating too much fat.

There is another way to prevent free-radical reactions in the body. Researchers are experimenting on the use of antioxidants, chemicals that tie up the reactive free radicals before they can damage the body's molecules. Adding antioxidants to the daily diet of experimental animals, from fruit flies and roundworms to mice, has produced increases of up to 30 percent in their life spans. Manufacturers have been adding one of these antioxidants, BHT, to cereals and other processed foods for many years. Unlike some food additives, which have turned out to be harmful to health,

BHT may actually be helping to lengthen our lives. Another common antioxidant is vitamin E, which occurs naturally in foods.

Researchers are also trying to prevent or reverse the effects of free-radical reactions, such as cross-linking and the formation of age pigments. Johan Bjorksten, who originated the cross-linkage theory of aging, has been searching for microorganisms that can dissolve the cross-linked biomolecules from aged animals. He has isolated enzymes that can dissolve insoluble fractions prepared from various human tissues. Preliminary tests of one of these enzymes on mice gave promising results, lengthening their lives and making them stronger and more active. A substance called beta-aminopropionitrile, found in the chick-pea, prevents the cross-linking of collagen. It may be useful in preventing wrinkled skin, stiffened joints, and other effects of aging.

The group of brain conditions sometimes called senility is another effect of aging that researchers are trying to prevent. Although such diseases affect only a small fraction of old people, they are probably the thing that people fear most about growing old. A drug called centrophenoxine has been used in Europe to improve the symptoms of senility in humans. It is now being tested in the United States. This chemical slows down the formation of the age pigment that builds up in nerve cells of aging animals.

Another chemical that decreases the accumulation of age pigment in the brain is dimethylaminoethanol (DMAE). DMAE is a natural body chemical. It stabilizes the membrane of the lysosomes, tiny structures inside the body cells that contain powerful decomposing enzymes. Some gerontologists think that as people age, their lysosome membranes become leaky, and their enzymes slip out into the cell. The powerful chemicals then damage cell structures and may be a key factor in the aging process. In experiments on mice, DMAE produced a 27 percent increase in their average lifetime.

Paul Gordon and his associates at Strategic Medical Research Corporation in Chicago have been studying the destructive changes that occur in aging cells. They are especially interested in the ribosomes, the tiny structures involved in making proteins. Gordon's team of researchers has been developing and testing drugs that help to rebuild the cell structures and at least partly reverse the changes that occur in aging. They have had promising results with a chemical called isoprinosine. This drug makes the ribosomes younger and makes the brains of aged animals work better. So far there has been some argument on whether the drug also helps aging humans. But many people may be taking isoprinosine soon. In addition to its antiaging properties, it is also a powerful virus-killing drug. It has not yet been approved for use in the United States, but it is being used in many other parts of the world. As old people take isoprinosine for virus infections, doctors will have more opportunities to observe its effects on aging as well.

This is an exciting time in aging research. Experiments like the ones described and many more are casting new light on what makes people age and suggesting effective ways to stop and reverse aging. Some gerontologists believe that we may soon be able to turn back the clock of life and keep people young as long as they live.

We are also gaining growing control over diseases. During this century, a variety of drugs, especially the antibiotics, have reduced bacterial diseases from a leading cause of death to a rather minor hazard. Worldwide vaccination has wiped smallpox from the face of the earth. New insights into cancer, heart disease, and the other major killers are unfolding, and researchers believe that we can conquer them, too.

If diseases that kill are conquered, and researchers learn how to stop aging, what will people die of? Some scientists believe that the question should be, "*Will* people continue to die?" And some of them believe that the answer is "No." They foresee a time—perhaps not very far off—when occasional accidents will be the only causes of death, and people will have life spans in the hundreds or even thousands of years!

A World Growing Old

MICHELANGELO, ONE OF THE GREATEST ARTISTIC geniuses of the Italian Renaissance, was seventy-one when he was appointed chief architect for the great St. Peter's Cathedral in Rome. For the next eighteen years he worked hard on the job, designing the main body of the church, supervising the builders, and painting huge frescoes on the walls of the Pauline Chapel. He also found time to write beautiful poetry. He was still working actively when he died in 1564 at the age of eighty-nine.

Benjamin Franklin—writer, scientist, inventor, statesman—had a long and active life, but some of his greatest achievements came in his later years. He was seventy when he helped to draft the Declaration of Independence and seventy-five when he helped to negotiate the peace between America and Great Brittain. At the age of eighty-one he played a key role in the creation of the United States Constitution.

Giuseppe Verdi, a famous composer of the nineteenth century, wrote two of his best operas when he was in his seventies. *Falstaff*, written when he was nearly eighty, was a comedy full of life and laughter. At eighty-four Verdi finished his *Stabat Mater*, a great choral work.

Thomas Alva Edison patented a total of 1,033 inventions that helped to shape our modern world. His patents, which covered such inventions as the electric light bulb, the microphone, and the phonograph, covered a span of sixty years, until he was eighty-one.

Margaret Mead, a noted anthropologist, made her first important study in New Guinea at the age of twenty-four. In 1973, when she was seventy-two, she went back to study the New Guinea natives again, living and working under primitive conditions. Three years later, a television crew filming a typical week in her life was exhausted following her around in her strenuous work schedule.

Margaret Mead, renowned anthropologist and curator of New York's American Museum of Natural History, was active in many areas right up until her death at the age of 76.

In ancient Greece the average life expectancy was only twenty years. According to records in Germany, the average life expectancy there in 1760 was about thirty-four years. In the Western world today the average life expectancy is seventy-three years, and it is increasing each year. Yet there have always been old people who lived to their seventies, eighties, nineties, or even longer. The difference is that now there are many more of them, and each year their number increases. In 1900, persons over sixty-five amounted to 4 percent of the United States population; now it is 10 percent.

It seems ironic that now, when there are more old people than ever before, the majority of them do not have an active role to play in society. There are a number of reasons for this strange and tragic situation.

Over the past few generations there has been a sweeping change in the nature of the family. A few generations ago, the "extended family" was rather common. Grandparents often lived with their children and grandchildren. An uncle or aunt might also live in the household. Extended families provided a secure role in life for the older members. The grandparents were considered wise, and their advice was sought in solving family problems. They helped to train the younger members of the family in useful household tasks, and sometimes in their occupations as well. When parents were too busy, there were always older family members around to tell a story or dry a child's tears.

The car and other advances in transportation and communication have now made us a mobile society. People move often, across town or across the country, looking for better jobs or living conditions. Houses and apartments are usually too small to hold three generations comfortably. The typical family has now become what is called the nuclear family. It consists of just two generations: parents and children. When the children grow up, they expect to set out on their own, whether they marry or not. As the parents age, they have only each other for close companionship. If one dies, the other is alone.

Another important factor in the changing role of the aged has been the growth and spread of retirement plans. Most working people today make regular contributions to a government-sponsored pension plan through deductions from their wages. When they retire, these payments entitle them to receive checks that are supposed to provide a minimum amount to live on. Many private companies have their own retirement plans in addition, which provide for a larger retirement income. People who save over the years, in banks or investments, have additional income for their retirement years.

The basic idea behind retirement plans was a very wise and humane one. It seemed unfair for a person who had worked for nearly a whole lifetime and then become too old and feeble to work not to have anything to live on. Old people commonly used to be provided for by their children or other family members. But with families no longer living together in the same household, this became difficult, and it was necessary for the community to provide some support for the aged.

However, what started out as a good idea became unfair in its own way. Retirement gradually changed from an opportunity to an obligation. People who continued to work after official retirement lost part or all of their Social Security benefits if their earnings were over a certain amount. In addition, many companies set up mandatory retirement programs, meaning that people *had* to retire whether they wanted to or not. In America in 1978, when Congress raised the mandatory retirement age to seventy for most occupations, there was a furious debate. Some people claimed that this measure would have a terrible effect on the economy. They said that people had a duty to retire at sixty-five; otherwise there would not be enough jobs for young people, and middle-aged executives would have no hope of getting promoted if the old people stayed on an extra five years.

Yet there is nothing magical about the age sixty-five. People are not young and active the day before their sixty-fifth birthday and then doddering old fossils a day later. Study after study has shown that in many types of jobs old people are just as efficient workers as younger ones (sometimes more so), and they are not particularly likely to miss many days of work because of illness. With medical advances helping more and more people to live longer and keeping them younger and more able, this kind of discrimination grows more and more unfair with each passing year. Older people have a lifetime of experience to draw upon. What a waste it is when we do not use their talents!

Pablo Picasso was a brilliant artist who very quickly became one of the best in his trade. He continued to create magnificent paintings and remained one of the greatest artists of all time throughout his life, working long hours that would be too much for most people years younger. He worked tirelessly for seventy-five years, creating masterpiece after masterpiece until his death at the age of ninety-one. How much poorer the world would have been if Picasso had been forced to retire at sixty-five.

Playwright George Bernard Shaw was still writing actively when he died at the age of ninety-four. Dr. Malley Kachel of Munich, Germany, was still working in medicine at the age of ninety-four. Duncan MacLean retired as a house painter at the age of eighty, but continued his hobby of sprinting and won a silver medal at the 1975 World Veterans' Olympics in Canada, when he was ninety years old. He ran 200 meters in 44 seconds.

Forcing older people to retire is a loss for the world, but it may be even worse for the people themselves. Even with good retirement plans, the income of a retired person is usually much lower than it was when he or she was working. People used to living a comfortable life may suddenly find they have to watch every penny and do without many things they used to enjoy. Inflation eats away at the value of their savings, and sudden medical expenses—which are more likely to occur in the aging years—can wipe out savings entirely. Many old people are forced to live in dingy rooms in rundown areas and cannot afford to buy well-balanced, nutritious foods.

Even if finances are not a problem, many people who retire find that they simply don't know what to do with themselves. During the long years while they worked hard at a job they perhaps did not enjoy very much, they dreamed of sitting in the sun all day after they retired. They would finally get a chance to read all those books they wanted to, or play a lot of golf, or putter around fixing up the house, or travel a bit. For the first few weeks, retirement is all they ever dreamed. It is like a glorious vacation, which goes on and on with no end in sight. But after a while, they find themselves getting bored. They think wistfully back to the job they thought they didn't like and find themselves missing the work routine. The prospect of not being needed by anyone, not having anything specific to do, stretching on for the rest of their lives, seems like torture.

Some people never adjust successfully to retirement, especially if they were forced to retire rather than choosing to retire. They begin to waste away, become ill and senile, and die within a few years. But others find retirement years a rewarding time of life. Some retired people go on working on a part-time basis, either with their old employers or in some other field. Some go in for volunteer work. Hospitals, day-care units, political campaigns, and many other worthy causes can always use some extra hands and minds. Some retired people occupy themselves with hobbies. This type of adjustment is most successful when people continue a hobby they have been interested in for many years. Sometimes retirement offers an opportunity to turn a hobby into a second career.

Remember the sudden aging of the salmon after spawning? The pioneer work on this strange life cycle was done by Dr. O. H. Robertson in the early 1950s. Dr. Robertson was a microbiologist and medical researcher. He had a distinguished career. During World War I, he created the first blood bank. Later he did some important research on pneumonia. But in 1949 he reached retirement age and was forced to retire. Retirement freed Dr. Robertson to pursue another interest. His lifetime hobby was fishing, and he had often wondered about the mysterious travels and dramatic death of the salmon. He began to travel with the fish and study them. He discovered one breed, the kokanee, that spends its whole life in land-locked lakes, yet still degenerates and dies right after spawning. Concentrating on this breed, because it was easy to keep track of during its entire life cycle, he observed and experimented. It was hard work. Once he performed delicate surgery on 200 tiny fish at the Lake Tahoe hatchery, and then a raccoon ate up most of his experiment. He continued to work and eliminated one possibility after another. Finally he discovered that the salmon's spectacular death is due to a massive malfunction of the hormone systems. When it is time to spawn, the salmon's adrenal and pituitary glands suddenly grow larger and go wildly out of control, producing a flood of hormones that cause the aging changes in the fish's body. Dr. Robertson announced his findings in 1953. He probably worked even harder on his salmon research than he did when he was working for pay as a microbiologist.

Where should old people live? That is a growing problem for many families today. Sometimes elderly parents come to live with their grown children, who may be raising growing families of their own. Sometimes the arrangement works out well, with the older generation providing help and wisdom that can benefit the whole family. But often difficult adjustments must be made. Both the parents and the grandparents have been used to leading their own lives and running their own homes. They have their own ways of doing things, and compromises are necessary to prevent constant clashes. Space may be a problem, and resentments may grow—a child resentful at having to give up his own room for grandma, and a grandparent unhappy after leaving a spacious home for a cramped room in someone else's house.

Many old people move to retirement communities. These may provide a variety of useful facilities and services, such as sturdy handgrips next to bathtubs and toilets, ramps for wheelchairs, convenient entertainments and activities, and a medical staff able to treat the problems of aging. But many of these communities are restricted to old people. Retired people may look forward to being away from the annoyance of noisy and mischievous children. But the company of nobody but old people can get boring. It has been found that people stay mentally alert and physically active and vigorous longer when they live in a community that has a mixture of people of different ages and occupations. Even more important is having friends and acquaintances and a role in the community. Moving can be difficult and upsetting.

Illness can bring even more upsets and problems, especially if it results in the person's being put in a hospital or a nursing home. Being suddenly ripped away from familiar possessions that recall the memories of a lifetime, having to adapt to strange people and rigid routines, and having frightening things done to your body can be terribly upsetting. Sometimes hospitalization of old people even results in a temporary mental illness.

Even when a hospital or nursing home is well run, the patients may become dependent and less able to live by themselves. But some nursing homes and retirement homes are a scandal. They are run by unscrupulous people who are only interested in the money they make, and staffed by untrained workers who don't care about the people for whom they are supposed to provide care. Investigations have revealed that patients sometimes are heavily drugged to keep

them from "making trouble." Tighter regulations are making the care for old people in such institutions better. But many gerontologists now believe that it is best to get elderly patients back into the community. Halfway houses, day-care units for the aged, and visiting nurse and homemaker services are helping to make this possible.

The 1960s and 1970s have been decades of crusades for minority rights. Recently the growing numbers of senior citizens, especially in the United States, have been discovering that they are a powerful political force. They have the leisure time to campaign for issues that affect them, and they can get out the votes. The National Council of Senior Citizens and the American Association of Retired Persons each number about three million members. A newer and more vocal organization, formed to fight for the rights of old people, is the Gray Panthers. This nonprofit organization was started in 1970 by Philadelphian Maggie Kuhn. Its activities have included testifying to Congress in favor of a national health service and picketing for consumers' rights. Maggie Kuhn declares, "Our society wants to keep the elderly out of the way, playing bingo and shuffleboard. . . . We are not mellowed, sweet old people. We're outraged, but we're doing something about it."

Maggie Kuhn, founder of the Gray Panthers organization, is seen here with the former mayor of Philadelphia, Joseph Clark, exerting some of her political clout.

Further Reading

READERS AND THEIR FAMILIES WHO WOULD LIKE more information about aging may find the following adult books interesting and helpful:

Comfort, Alex. *A Good Age*. New York: Crown Publishers, 1976.

Curtin, Sharon. *Nobody Ever Died of Old Age*. Boston: Little, Brown and Company, 1972.

Knopf, Olga. *Successful Aging*. New York: Viking Press, 1975.

Kurtzman, Joel, and Gordon, Philip. *No More Dying*. Los Angeles: J. P. Tarcher, 1976.

Lamb, Marion J. *Biology of Ageing*. New York: John Wiley and Sons, 1977.

Puner, Morton. *To the Good Long Life*. New York: Universe Books, 1974.

Rosenfeld, Albert. *Prolongevity*. New York: Alfred A. Knopf, 1976.

Segerberg, Osborn, Jr. *The Immortality Factor*. New York: E. P. Dutton and Company, 1974.

Stonecypher, D. D., Jr. *Getting Older and Staying Young*. New York: W. W. Norton and Company, 1974.

Strehler, Bernard L. *Time, Cells, and Aging*. 2nd ed. New York: Academic Press, 1977.

Winter, Ruth. *Ageless Aging*. New York: Crown Publishers, 1973.

Index

Age pigment, 44–45, 64–65
"Age spots" on skin, 23
Aging, characteristics of, 17–29
Aging and continuous growth, 9–10
Aging in lower organisms, 8–10
Aging, myths, 46
Air pollution, 29
American Association of Retired Persons, 79
Amino acids, 58
Antioxidants, 63–64
Appetite, 26
Arthritis, 29
Aslan, Ana, 54
Autoimmune reactions, 43

BHT, 63–64
Bacteria, 8

Baldness, 23
Baruch, Bernard, 2
Beta-aminopropionitrile, 64
Bicycling, 30
Bimini, 49
Biological clock, 13–14, 60
Bjorksten, Johan, 64
Bodenstein, Dietrich, 60–61
Brain, 27–28, 60
Brain weight and life span, 15–16
Breath, shortness of, 25
Bristlecone pines, 10
Brown-Séquard, Charles Edouard, 50–51
Bubb, Cora and Phil, 17–18
Burnet, F. MacFarlane, 37

Calcium deposits, 24

Cancer, 29, 31
Cartilage, 24
Caucasus, 33–34
Cell division, 8–9, 38–39
Centenarians, 3, 32–36
Centrophenoxine, 64
Chimpanzee, 13
China, 47–48
Cholesterol, 61
Churchill, Winston, 4, 21, 54
Cockroach, 60–61
Collagen, 23–24, 64
Colon, 53
Cornaro, Luigi, 49
Craftwork, 40
Cross-linking, 24, 44, 64

David, King, 47
de Gaulle, Charles, 54
"Death hormone," 42–43, 60
Denckla, W. Donner, 42
Depression, 28
Diabetes, 29, 31
Diet restriction, 56, 58–59
Digestive problems, 25
Dimethylaminoethanol
  (DMAE), 64–65
Diseases of old age, 29, 59
Dog, 15

Edison, Thomas Alva, 68
Elephant, 15
Environmental causes of ag-
  ing, 43–44
Enzymes, 64, 65
Eos, 46
Error catastrophe, 44
Exercise programs for the
  aged, 29, 30
84)

Extended family, 70
Eyes, changes in, 19–20

Fibroblast, 38–39
Financial problems of the
  aged, 73–74
Forman, Sylvia, 36
Fountain of youth, 48–49
Franklin, Benjamin, 67–68
Free radicals, 44, 62–64
Fruit flies, 63

Gene, 37
Genetic programming of ag-
  ing, 38–39, 41
Georgia (Soviet), 33–34
Gerontology, 6
Gerovital H₃, 54
Gordon, Paul, 65
Gorilla, 13
Gray Panthers, 79
Graying of hair, 23
Greek myths, 46–48

Halfway houses, 79
Harman, Denham, 44, 62
Hayflick, Leonard, 38–39
Hearing loss, 20–22
Heart, 25, 29, 44
Heart disease, 29, 31, 62–63
Hera, 48
Homemaker services, 79
Hormones, 50–52, 60, 62
Hormones and aging, 42–43
Hunza, 33–34
Hypothalamus, 41–42, 60

Immune system, 29, 43, 59–60, 62
Inactivity, effects of, 24

Incontinence, 25
Indian legends, 48–49
Infectious diseases, 29–31
Inflation, 74
Intelligence and aging, 26
Isoprinosine, 65

Joints, stiffness of, 24, 64
Juvenile hormone, 61

Kachel, Malley, 73
Kidneys, 29, 59
Khrushchev, Nikita, 54
Kuhn, Maggie, 78, 79

Lactobacilli, 53
Lansing, Albert, 15
Leaf, Alexander, 33
Life expectancy, 2, 65, 70
Life span, 2, 3, 11–16, 56, 61–64
Liu, Richard, 59
Ludwig, Frederic C., 61
Lungs, 29, 59
Lysosomes, 65

MacLean, Duncan, 73
Mandeville, Sir John, 48
Mazess, Richard B., 34
McCay, Clive, 56
Mead, Margaret, 68, 69
Medvedev, Zhores, 34
Memory, 27
Menopause, 26, 42
Mental confusion, 28
Metabolic rate and life span, 15
Metchnikoff, Elie, 53–54
Michelangelo, 67
Miller, D. S., 56, 58
Monsanto Corporation, 58

Moses, Anna Mary (Grandma), 4, 5
Mouse, 11, 15, 62–65

National Council of Senior Citizens, 79
National Institute on Aging, 56
Nervous system, 26
Niehans, Paul, 54
Novocain, 54
Nuclear family, 71
Nursing homes, 77, 79

Obesity, 26
On-off switches of genes, 39, 41
Orgel, Leslie, 43
Osteoporosis, 24
Ovaries, 42
Oxygen, 44, 62

Parabiosis, 60–61
Paracelsus, 49
Payne, P. R., 56, 58
Personality changes, 28
Picasso, Pablo, 35, 73
Pituitary, 42, 60
Ponce de León, 49
Pope Innocent VIII, 47
Progeria, 36–37
Protein, 58
Protozoa, 8, 9

Radiation damage to genes, 43
Rat, 16, 42, 58, 59, 62
Redwood trees, 10
Regeneration, 9
Research on aging, 55–66
Research on aging Act, 56
Retirement age, 2, 72

85)

Retirement, adjustment to, 74–77
Retirement communities, 76–77
Retirement plans, 71–72
Ribosomes, 65
Robertson, O. H., 75–76
Rome, ancient, 47
Roundworms, 63
Royal jelly, 54

Sacher, George, 15
Salmon, 11, 75–76
Sandburg, Carl, 6, 57
Schweitzer, Albert, 4, 12
Sea anemone, 9–10
Senility, 27–28, 64
Senior citizens organizations, 79
Sensation, loss of, 22–23
Serotonin, 60
Sex life and aging, 26
Shaw, George Bernard, 73
Shock, Nathan, 45
Size and life span, 14–15
Skin, changes in, 23
Smoking, aging effect of, 23
Social Security, 72
Sponge, 9
Squirrel, 15–16
Steinach, Eugen, 51
Stokowski, Leopold, 6
Strehler, Bernard, 39, 55
Strength, decrease in, 24–25
Stroke, 28
Sturgeon, 10
Syria, ancient, 47

Taoism, 47–48
Taste, loss of, 22
Teeth, 25

Temperature control, 23
Temperature, effect on aging, 43, 59–60
Testicles, 50–52
Testosterone, 51
Theories of aging, 37–45
Thymosin, 62
Thymus, 43, 62
Thyroid, 42
Timiras, Paola S., 60
Tithonus, 46
Tortoises, 10
Trees, 10
Tryptophan, 58
Turtles, 10

Unsaturated fats, 44, 62–63

Vas deferens, 51
Vasectomy, 51
Verdi, Giuseppe, 68
Vilcabamba, 33–34, 36
Virus infections, 65
Visiting nurse services, 79
Vitamin E, 64
Voronoff, Serge, 51–52

Walford, Roy, 59
Work efficiency of the aged, 72–73
World Veterans' Olympics, 73
Wright, Frank Lloyd, 4
Wrinkling, 23, 64

Yeast, 8
Yogurt, 53–54

Zeus, 46, 48

DATE DUE